Your Book, Your Buzz

A NO-B.S. GUIDE TO BUILDING BUZZ AROUND YOUR BOOK

(without selling your soul)

MEGS THOMPSON

INTUITIVE WRITING COACH, WORD-TWERKING
BOOK-DOULA, GHOSTWRITER & PUBLISHER

www.inomniaparatuspublishing.com

Table of Contents

Congratulations!

Seriously, you wrote a book - that's a really big deal & something you should be celebrating.

That being said, now it's time to start TELLING people about the amazing book you wrote - otherwise, your magic is going to sit on the shelf, not receiving the appreciation & attention it deserves.

As an Intuitive Writing Coach, Word-Twerking Book-Doula, Ghostwriter, Editor & Publisher, I spend the majority of my time talking with people who are in one of three positions:

1 - they have an idea or a dream about writing a book
2 - they've written a book & it's about to be published
3 - they wrote & published their book but feel like it fell flat & want a do-over!

The great thing about writing a book is that once it's written, it's done. You never have to write that first book again. But, once it's been published & is out there in the world, you can always re-start the buzz around your brilliance - boosting book sales, excitement & expanding your audience of readers.

As much as you can, try not to stress about numbers, likes, comments, shares, views, etc. Instead, feel into the emotions that come up throughout this process & journal about everything you're thinking & feeling. Celebrate EVERYTHING. Every. Single. Tiny. Thing. Because no matter how 'woo' or crazy it might sound, that energy will attract more of the same.

Then, as much as you're comfortable, share your excitement on social media, with your email list & during in-person interactions. There is NO such thing as too much excitement or sharing. Writing a book is such a huge accomplishment and something to be incredibly proud of. You are basically a ROCK STAR. You've done something that less than 1% of people will actually do during their lifetime! Nearly everyone you'll meet says that they want to write a book *trust me*, but less than 3% will & less than 1% of those folks will actually publish their book. So, it's important that you recognize yourself for what you've done.

This guide is your roadmap, your hype crew, your permission slip & your gentle kick in the butt—all wrapped into one. Think of it like having me in your corner, whispering *(or occasionally shouting)*, "You've got this!" while handing you tools that actually make a difference.

You don't have to do everything in here *(& definitely not all at once)*, but everything you'll find is here to support your success—as an author, as a brand & as a beautiful human with something worth sharing.

Skim, highlight, post-it, scribble, dog-ear, or jump around—this guide is here for you however you need it.

Now, you may be wondering - Who are you?!

I'm Megs & I've been helping uniquely creative badasses just like you birth their books, share their stories & build brands that feel like soul-truth confetti for years. I'm an Intuitive Writing Coach, Word-Twerking Book-Doula, Ghostwriter, Editor & Publisher who believes deeply in the power of storytelling as a path to healing, connection & massive visibility.

I've walked this road with over 100 authors *(so far)* from all walks of life, at all stages of the writing journey. I know where things get sticky, where self-doubt sneaks in & where we all tend to overthink *(or under-celebrate)*. So, everything in this guide is infused with experience, intuition, strategy & a healthy dose of loving *"get it done, gorgeous"* energy.

One last note before you get going... Remember that just as with everything else in life, there is no one-size-fits-all book marketing strategy. And that's a good thing. What works for someone else might feel heavy or misaligned for you. This guide isn't here to add pressure; it's here to spark ideas, offer tools & help you take confident, clear, aligned steps forward—your way.

Give yourself permission to try things, tweak things, skip things & circle back later. Want to shout about your book every day? Amazing. Want to whisper it from the mountaintop with a soft graphic & a dreamy caption? Also amazing. Go at your own pace, trust your gut & don't forget: this gets to feel good. **After all, you wrote a book!**

Your Author Brand: Where You & Your Book Begin

Let's start with a little truth bomb: *Your book is not your brand— you are.*

Yes, your book is magical. Yes, it deserves love & attention & gold foil bookmarks with your name on them. But your brand as an author? That's built around your voice, your values, your vibe. It's the energy you bring into a room—virtual or otherwise. It's what your readers feel when they read your posts, see your book cover, or hear you talk about why this story needed to be told. So, let's talk about that.

Building Your Identity as an Author

Here's the thing: you don't need to pretend to be someone else to be a "real author." You don't need fancy glasses, a moody aesthetic, or a book nook filled with neutral-toned throw blankets (*though... let's be real, if you've got one, invite me over*).

Your author identity is a reflection of YOU. The version of you who wrote this book. The version of you who decided to publish your book even when you were scared. The version of you who has something to say & knows it matters.

Ask yourself:

- What themes or messages do I naturally return to?

- What do I want my readers to feel when they engage with me or my writing?

- How do I want to show up in the world—as a storyteller, creator & human?

Your "author brand" isn't a logo or a curated color palette (*though those can help reinforce it*). It's the trust & energy people associate with your name. It's consistency, clarity & connection—all wrapped up in your unique flavor. So, show up fully & let your readers know the human behind the words. They aren't just buying your book, they're buying into your world.

Community > Vanity Metrics

We are not here for the follower-count Olympics. You don't need 10,000 Instagram followers or a blue check mark to be a successful, visible & connected author. What you do need is a community that feels like yours, people who care about you & readers who feel seen, heard, or transformed by what you share— whether it's a page from your book or a post about the iced coffee you just spilled all over your laptop.

Vanity metrics are just that—flashy numbers that look good on the surface but don't actually guarantee engagement, connection, or book sales. So instead of chasing followers, focus on nurturing your community.

- Respond to comments & DMs.
- Ask questions & actually care about the answers.
- Share your process, your quirks, your joy, your bloopers.
- Let people in & they'll stick around.

A reader who feels connected to you is far more valuable than 100 who just scrolled past a pretty post. So build your brand on belonging, not broadcasting.

The Long Game: Connection Over Conversion

Look, I get it. When you've poured your heart into writing & publishing a book, of course, you want people to buy it. Of course, you want sales, reviews, features, fan art & for your book to show up in someone's BookTok stack.

But here's the soul-truth: Sustainable success as an author comes from connection, not conversion. Don't let your online presence become one long "Buy My Book!" echo chamber. Instead, use your content to connect, your energy to invite & your story to build trust, spark conversation & remind your readers that they matter to you—whether they buy or not.

Some people will follow you for months—or years—before they ever buy a book & that's okay. Some readers will become lifelong fans after one short story. Some podcast interviews will spark something you never saw coming. The point is: you're planting seeds, building momentum & creating a space where people want to support you, not because you pushed a sale, but because you showed up as YOU.

TLDR

- Your book is part of your brand, but YOU are the center of it.
- Ditch the numbers game & build real relationships.
- Focus on creating value, sharing honestly & showing up with heart.
- You don't need to be *everywhere*; you need to be where it feels most authentic & aligned for you, your book & your brand.

Your energy is magnetic, your voice is already enough & your author brand is being built every time you choose to show up on purpose, as your whole, authentic, book-writing self.

Notes & Sparks of Genius:

_____

_____

_____

_____

_____

_____

_____

_____

_____

_____

_____

_____

_____

_____

_____

_____

_____

_____

Notes & Sparks of Genius:

_____

_____

_____

_____

_____

_____

_____

_____

_____

_____

_____

_____

_____

_____

_____

_____

_____

_____

_____

_____

_____

_____

_____

_____

_____

_____

_____

_____

Social Media Magic
(No Dance Moves Required)

There are no shortage of social media platforms available & by the time this book is published, there may even be a few more that have popped up. I've included a quick overview of some of the more popular platforms below as a quick refresher. I recommend that my clients focus their attention on two platforms *(three at most)*, instead of trying to tackle them all.

When making that decision for yourself, keep in mind where your readers & audience are going to be spending their time, as well as where you feel most comfortable & like you'll be able to create content with ease & enjoyment. There are also multiple different ways to post on many of these platforms & different forms of content will connect & grab the attention of a different audience.

Because social media is changing constantly, it's always a good idea to do your own research as far as where YOUR people are spending their time.

- **TikTok** – this is for the younger audience *(Gen Z & Millennials)*
- **Instagram** *(IG)* – this is for quite a few audiences, but keep in mind the focus is going to be heavily visual *(photos, stories & reels)* as opposed to copy or text, so it usually draws a different audience than Facebook or Reddit.
- **Facebook** *(FB)* – here you can balance that visual element with written posts while still having stories & reels like IG, but you have the added benefit of FB groups *(there are literally TONS of virtual book clubs hosted in FB Groups)*
- **Reddit** – this is a great space if you're writing niche-fiction & is home to fandoms galore.
- **Pinterest** – often overlooked, Pinterest in actually the #1 search engine for women, so if your audience is primarily women & you're writing non-fiction, self-help, personal development, parenting, etc. Pinterest may be the place for you.
- **LinkedIn** *(LI)*- this is the go-to social media networking platform for professionals, so if your book is heavily focused on business, LinkedIn may be your spot.

At the end of the day, it's important to remember that what you're creating through your social media presence is a community of readers & fans not only of your books, but of you & the brand you're creating as an author. This doesn't always correlate to book sales, however, it does a *ton* of heavy lifting when it comes to getting your book into the right hands, in front of the right people & getting you on the right stages.

Notes & Sparks of Genius:

Quick & East Value-Packed Social Media Post Ideas

When you're looking at this list of topics & ideas, keep in mind that for each 'post' you write, you can repurpose that same content as a reel, a story, a quick video, a poll, etc. This is a great way to work smarter/not harder & ensure that you're connecting with every facet of your audience.

Book-Focused Posts
(*Keep your book top-of-mind without feeling repetitive or sleezy.*)
- "Here's a little teaser from Chapter [X]" (*include 1–2 juicy sentences*)
- "3 books that inspired this one"
- "Where I was in life when I started writing this book"
- "The first idea that popped into my head for this book (*and how it changed)*"
- "If my book were a movie, here's the cast I'd dream of"
- Flatlay photo of your book next to coffee, candles, or anything cozy
- "What readers have said about my book so far" (*ARC reviews, testimonials, DMs*)
- A closer look at a line, scene, or character that means a lot to you—and why
- "I just hit [milestone]!" (*first sale, first review, book birthday, etc*)
- "Here's what came in my book shipment today!" (*unboxing-style*)

Writers-Life Posts
(*Let them see the process, not just the end result.*)
- "My writing space today" (*messy desk? bed? parked car? It's all content*)
- "My weird little writing rituals" (*candles, snacks, lucky socks, etc*)
- "What I'm listening to while writing"
- Share a favorite writing quote & reflect on it
- "Here's what a typical writing day looks like for me"
- "One thing I struggled with while writing this book"
- "One part of this book that came out exactly how I wanted it to"
- "What's fueling me while I write today" (*coffee order, snack, comfort food*)
- "Writing tool/product I swear by" (*an app, a planner, a certain pen, etc.*)
- "The lie I believed about writing for way too long"

Lifestyle Posts
(Show who you are outside of the book—and let your people fall in love with you.)
- "My current morning (or evening) routine in 3 words"
- "Little things bringing me joy this week"
- Photo dump from a recent walk, hike, or outing
- "What I do when I'm stuck on a scene" (movement, music, snacks, etc.)
- Your fave cozy writing outfit or accessories
- "What I'm watching when I should be writing"
- Pet or plant update *(your dog/cat/fern = recurring side character!)*
- "My go-to way to decompress after a big writing sprint"
- "Where I run to when I need a reset"
- "My author day off looks like..."

Personality & Fun Facts Posts
(Let your audience get to know you like a friend—not just their favorite author.)
- "3 fun facts about me (that have nothing to do with writing)"
- "High school me would be shocked to know I..."
- "Something totally random I'm irrationally afraid of"
- "What I'm totally obsessed with right now"
- "My current hyperfixation playlist (no judgment please)"
- "If I weren't writing books, I'd probably be ____"
- "Impulse purchase I don't regret at all"
- "My comfort meal when I'm in a mood"
- "Where I'd go for a solo writing retreat if money/time didn't matter"
- "Unpopular opinion: _____"

Random & Interactive Posts
(Lighthearted posts to entertain, engage, and build connection.)
- This or That: Coffee vs Tea, Pen vs Keyboard, Sunrise vs Sunset, etc.
- Mood board or aesthetic for your book, your main character, or your life
- "Ask me anything" post or Q&A box
- "What's on your TBR right now?" *(Ask your followers + share yours)*
- "Caption this photo" *(a funny or awkward writing moment pic)*
- "My writing mascot for today" *(real pet or silly object)*
- "What do you think happens next?" *(Post a story snippet and ask for guesses)*
- "First draft vs final version" *(share a before/after of a sentence or idea)*

Notes & Sparks of Genius:

_____

_____

_____

_____

_____

_____

_____

_____

_____

_____

_____

_____

_____

_____

_____

_____

_____

_____

_____

_____

_____

_____

_____

_____

_____

_____

Notes & Sparks of Genius:

_____
_____
_____
_____
_____
_____
_____
_____
_____
_____
_____
_____
_____
_____
_____
_____
_____
_____
_____
_____
_____
_____
_____
_____
_____
_____

Notes & Sparks of Genius:

_____

_____

_____

_____

_____

_____

_____

_____

_____

_____

_____

_____

_____

_____

_____

_____

_____

_____

_____

_____

_____

_____

_____

_____

_____

_____

_____

Notes & Sparks of Genius:

Sample Social Media Content Calendar

For this sample plan, I've chosen to focus on Facebook & Instagram as my two social media platforms. I also like to prioritize being offline as much as possible on the weekends so I don't schedule anything for those days. I like to write my posts first, then create a short reel & story that uses the same content, recorded in my own voice or as captions with a catchy song & a slideshow of my own photos or a quick video clip. This is a great way to connect with different members of my audience without doing double the work.

Monday:
- Post to FB & IG wall/page re: a moment of magic from the weekend
- Post Reel & Story to FB & IG re: a moment of magic from the weekend

Tuesday:
- Post to FB & IG wall/page re: where I'd go for a dream solo writing retreat
- Post Reel & Story to FB & IG re: where I'd go for a dream solo writing retreat

Wednesday:
- Post to FB & IG wall/page re: typical day in the life
- Post Reel & Story to FB & IG re: typical day in the life

Thursday:
- Post to FB & IG wall/page re: ask me anything about my writing/creative process
- Post Reel & Story to FB & IG re: ask me anything about my writing/creative process

Friday:
- Post to FB & IG wall/page re: my dream cast if/when my book becomes a movie
- Post Reel & Story to FB & IG re: my dream cast if/when my book becomes a movie

Create Your Own Social Media Content Calendar:

Mondays:

- _____
- _____

Tuesdays:

- _____
- _____

Wednesdays:

- _____
- _____

Thursdays:

- _____
- _____

Fridays:

- _____
- _____

Saturdays:

- _____
- _____

Sundays:

- _____
- _____

Create Your Own Social Media Content Calendar:

Mondays:
- _____
- _____

Tuesdays:
- _____
- _____

Wednesdays:
- _____
- _____

Thursdays:
- _____
- _____

Fridays:
- _____
- _____

Saturdays:
- _____
- _____

Sundays:
- _____
- _____

Create Your Own Social Media Content Calendar:

Mondays:

- _____
- _____

Tuesdays:

- _____
- _____

Wednesdays:

- _____
- _____

Thursdays:

- _____
- _____

Fridays:

- _____
- _____

Saturdays:

- _____
- _____

Sundays:

- _____
- _____

Email List Love Affair

If you've ever spent any time marketing a business *(yours or someone else's)*, you understand how valuable it is to have an audience of YOUR people who've opted into hearing from you on a regular basis. Not to mention, we never know what's going to happen with a social media platform from day to day, so being able to have a captive audience that you have complete control over & access to at all times, is invaluable. *Remember the last time Meta crashed & every small business owner in the world lost their shit because they had no way of contacting their audience?! Having an email list is the best way to combat that headache.*

The easiest way to start developing this audience is to create something YOUR people desire. This may be a sneak peak of your upcoming book, the first chapter, behind the scenes insights from a 'day in the life' of their soon-to-be favorite author, printable goodies like bookmarks, desktop backgrounds, phone wallpapers, interactive quizzes that get them involved in your stories/books/characters lives, etc. What matters is that it's something your readers are interested in & for them to receive it or gain access, they first have to opt-in to your email list.

Once someone has opted in to your email list, though, they're going to expect to hear from you, so be sure to mark a time on your calendar at least once a week to stay in touch. This can be as simple as a quick note to check in with them, let them know what you're up to, spill any exciting news, share places you may be visiting for live events, podcasts you'll be appearing on, or your newest favorite writing/reading tool.

Having an email list of subscribers may seem like a lot of work up-front but trust me, there's nothing like having 300, 400, or 5,000 people dying to know when your next book is coming out & where *they* can get their copy!

I recommend flipping back to the Social Media Content Calendar that you created in the last section & pencil in which day of the week you're going to start emailing your audience of adoring fans. Then, once you've chosen a day, you'll find a list of low-effort, high-value content ideas perfect for sending out via email, to keep your readers engaged between books, build connection & anticipation.

Notes & Sparks of Genius:

Low-effort, High-value Email Content Ideas

Writing Journey + Behind-the-Scenes
(Let your readers feel like insiders. People love getting a peek behind the curtain.)
- A short story about how the book idea came to you
- A photo of your writing space *(even if it's messy!)*
- A "writing ritual" you swear by *(candle, playlist, coffee order)*
- A behind-the-scenes of your book cover reveal process
- "3 things I'm googling for research right now"
- Screenshots of silly typos or edits with commentary
- A peek at a scene that almost made it in the book but didn't
- A draft title list or character name brainstorm you scrapped
- Your personal launch countdown checklist

Book-Adjacent Content
(A great way to add value without always talking about your book directly.)
- Bookmarks or phone wallpapers with quotes from your book
- Book recommendations—"If you liked my book, you might love..."
- A themed playlist inspired by your story or characters
- Character profiles or "interviews" with your main characters
- A 3-question book club discussion guide or journaling prompt
- Share your book's aesthetic board *(Pinterest or Canva style)*
- Share a favorite quote from your book with a quick reflection
- A fun "book trailer" GIF or Canva video you made

Personal Connection Points
(Let your audience get to know YOU as a human, not just a book-writing machine.)
- A quick note on what's lighting you up lately *(life, a good meal, a new read)*
- "3 things I'm obsessed with this week"
- A funny or vulnerable story about your publishing journey
- A Q&A box or poll *(ask them something & share the results next time)*
- A link to your favorite recent podcast episode or article
- Your current go-to writing snack or guilty pleasure
- A funny meme or quote that made your day *(bonus: tie it into your book)*
- A "life lately" photo dump or journal-style note

Audience Engagement/Value-Based
(Keep them involved & feeling like they matter.)

- Ask them to help choose between two cover fonts/colors *(via link or reply)*
- Invite them to submit questions for a future Q&A email
- Create a quick quiz *(e.g., "Which character are you?" or "Should you write a book?")*
- Exclusive sneak peek of your next chapter or project
- A printable reading tracker or "To Be Read" list template
- Early access to events *(book signings, virtual meetups, etc.)*
- Offer a "subscriber-only" short story or bonus epilogue
- Shoutout a reader or reviewer of the month

Bonus Pro Tips for Stellar Email Execution:

- Keep your emails short & scannable *(2–3 paragraphs max)*
- Use a repeatable format *(ex: "3 Things This Week" or "Behind the Book Friday")*
- Send emails consistently—don't ghost your readers!
- Use P.S. lines! They're actually the most-read part of most emails.
- Occasionally include a call to action: "Hit reply and tell me ___" People love being asked for their thoughts, especially when it's by someone they admire, like their favorite author.

Notes & Sparks of Genius:

_____

_____

_____

_____

_____

_____

_____

_____

_____

_____

_____

Notes & Sparks of Genius:

Notes & Sparks of Genius:

Your Author Website (AKA Your Digital Home Base)

Having a website for yourself as an author isn't a requirement by any means. Especially when you can already have mini-author-pages set up on various social media platforms. That being said, once you're getting ready to launch your new book, or your next book, having a single landing page where your readers *(new & old)* can find out when the book is being released, where you'll be doing signings, readings & how they can connect with you is a MUST!

This doesn't only make it easier for your readers either, having a single place where you can update everything is a huge timesaver for YOU as a busy author. My biggest words of advice are to take a look at some of your favorite authors, check out what they have available as their websites – the majority of these are going to be super simple landing pages without much fluff or glitter.

One of the quickest mini-author-pages you'll want to set up is your **Amazon Author Central Account.** The purpose of setting up your Author Central account is to enhance the professional appearance of your book listing on Amazon. Once you've set up your profile, Amazon will include your photo & a portion of your bio on the sales page for each of your books, which helps enhance your credibility & give your readers a glimpse into who you are. (*www.author.amazon.com*)

It's against Amazon's terms of service to request positive reviews, discourage people from leaving negative reviews, or compensate them with anything other than a free copy of the book. However, there's nothing wrong with requesting reviews from people who have a high probability of liking your book.

Another great mini-author-page to set up is with **GoodReads**. Goodreads is basically the go-to social network for readers, it's where people track what they're reading, build never-ending TBR piles, leave reviews & discover new authors. By claiming your author profile, you're giving readers an easy way to find your book, follow your work & engage with you in a space built for bookworms.

Having an accurate GoodReads author page also adds a layer of legitimacy to your brand, especially for potential readers, book bloggers, reviewers & book club hosts who want to learn more about you before diving into your work. Your Goodreads page doesn't need to be complicated, just a photo, a short bio & a link to your book. *(www.goodreads.com)*

A few other great free sites where you can create a mini-author-page are:

- **BookBub** *(www.bookbub.com)*
- **Reedsy** *(www.reedsy.com)*
- **BookSirens** *(www.booksirens.com)*
- **Medium** *(www.medium.com)*

If you do opt to create a formal author website, there are a few platforms that make creating a single landing page site as easy as 1-2-3.

- **Squarespace** *(www.squarespace.com)*
- **Kajabi** *(www.kajabi.com)*
- **Wix** *(www.wix.com)*

Notes & Sparks of Genius:

_____

_____

_____

_____

_____

_____

_____

_____

_____

_____

_____

Notes & Sparks of Genius:

Notes & Sparks of Genius:

_____
_____
_____
_____
_____
_____
_____
_____
_____
_____
_____
_____
_____
_____
_____
_____
_____
_____
_____
_____
_____
_____
_____
_____
_____
_____

From Lurkers to Lovers: Turning Attention Into Action

The Book Buzz Funnel *(aka the Date-to-Mate Model)*

Now it's time to start taking those lurkers from hiding on the outskirts of the action to falling in love with you, your book & your brand. Some may call this a 'funnel' – others like to think of it as a ladder. Personally? I like to think of it as a choose-your-own-adventure love story between you & your future readers. Essentially, it's about guiding the lovely humans who've:

- stumbled across your IG reels or FB page...
- clicked on your book teaser...
- joined your email list...
- lurked in your stories while sipping their morning latte...

...to take that next, delicious step of buying your book, reading it, loving it & maybe *(bless them)* shouting it out to their besties or book club.

Now, here's the part where most authors freeze. Funnels? Sounds techy. Ladders? Sounds like climbing. But trust me, it's way less "marketing bro" & way more "magnetic trail of bread crumbs" that leads straight to your book baby.

So, what does a beginner-friendly author funnel look like? Well, let's keep it cute, cozy & uncomplicated:

- **Step 1: Make a great first impression** *(Hi! I exist!)*
 This is your intro point; it could be a fun social post, a juicy blog article, a podcast interview, or even a Pinterest pin that leads them to your author website or freebie. Think of it as waving at your reader from across the room & flashing your bookish smile.

Tip: Share a sneak peek, a relatable quote, or a "behind-the-scenes" moment that's easy to connect with.

- **Step 2: Offer a delicious freebie** *(Come a little closer, darling.)*
Once you've grabbed their attention, give them a reason to stick around. This is where an opt-in gift comes in: a short story, a chapter preview, a quiz, a printable, or anything fun & value-packed that your ideal reader would adore.

Tip: Keep it relevant to your book or author vibe. Paranormal romance writer? Try a *"Which Book Boyfriend Are You?"* quiz. Self-help author? Offer a journaling prompt bundle.

- **Step 3: Nurture that budding relationship** *(We should hang out more.)*
Now that they're in your inbox, treat them like a new friend. Show up regularly, but not annoyingly, with value, personality & the occasional confetti-cannon of excitement about your book.

Tip: Schedule a weekly email or two a month with quick updates, reader Q&As, personal anecdotes, sneak peeks, etc. Be YOU. After all, that's who they came for.

- **Step 4: The ask** *(Want to take this to the next level?)*
This is where you invite them to buy your book. No begging. No pushy energy. Just a confident, joyful share: *"This thing I made is ready for you if you're ready for it."*

Tip: Make it easy. Include direct links, eye-catching graphics & social proof like ARC reviews or reader testimonials.

- **Step 5: Fan the flames** *(Tell your friends. Leave a review. Be my book hero.)*
Once someone becomes a reader, they're GOLD. So keep loving on them, thanking them & making it fun to be part of your book world. Invite them to leave reviews, tag you in posts, or join your next launch team.

Tip: Try posting a *"Reader Appreciation"* shoutout day on your social media platforms or offer fun bonus content to reviewers. Remember, you're building a community, not just selling a product.

Your funnel/ladder/whatever-you-want-to-call-it doesn't need to be fancy. It just needs to feel like YOU & create a clear, cozy path from "new to your world" to "can't wait to read your next book." The best part? Once you set it up, it starts working in the background, welcoming new readers, warming them up & making your launch *(& your legacy)* that much more powerful.

Building Awareness

Think of this step as your online dating profile or if you'd prefer to keep it professional, your online resume. This is where you get to provide fun snippets about who you are, what you like, what you don't, what you're looking for & what you're not. You're introducing yourself to your future readers & allowing them to get to know you without any pressure or requirements on their end, which makes it safe & invites them to feel comfortable observing you without interaction or expectations. This can be done in a number of ways. I've included some quick highlights here & we'll dig deeper into each of these areas a little later on.

- **Social Media Posts** – Those accounts we talked about before, make sure you're posting regularly. Now, that may be weekly, twice a week, or every other day – that's up to you, but once you've decided on your 'schedule' stick to it. Believe it or not, your audience will start to look forward to those posts & if you miss posting, they'll notice, whether they realize it or not and they'll start questioning your reliability. Remember, they haven't even agreed to give you their number or meet for coffee yet! First impressions matter. Don't only post about your book, though, talk about what you're reading, what author's get you excited, your favorite writing/reading tools, your favorite place to write, how you unplug/unwind, etc.

- **Social Media Ads** – If you're in a place financially where you'd like to look at running targeted ads to show your book cover, teasers, etc, you can do that. Personally, I recommend waiting to do this until you already have at least 1,000 followers or friends on your desired platform(s), simply because this helps you to have a more targeted audience & get better results. When you do decide to run ads, be sure you have a clear desire in mind *(ie. Increasing followers, directing to your website, gaining email subscribers, etc)* otherwise it becomes a shit/wall scenario which does nothing more than make a mess & cost you $$$.

- **Podcast Appearances** – I can't say enough about how much authors overlook the power of podcasts. There are hundreds of thousands of podcasts for & by authors & readers, meaning all you have to do is find a handful that fit your style, your genre, your audience, etc. If there's anything I've learned from building my businesses, it's the power of utilizing other people's audiences. Podcasts are a prime example of that. Think of it this way, if you do a single podcast interview every week, that's 4/month, 48/year. Those interviews are then available on various platforms around the interwebs, around the world & being shared by the podcast host. So really, most of the heavy lifting is being done FOR you. And, podcasts live on forever, just like your book. Have you ever thought about how much more you feel connected with someone you've been able to see or hear speak? As opposed to simply reading a blog or article they've written? There's just something extra magic about hearing a person's voice – *that's why audiobooks read by the author are such a big deal, too.*

- **Book Trailer Videos** – This can be really fun once your book is finished, the cover is designed & you're getting closer to your publication/launch date. There are a number of places to find professional creators *(You can definitely look at Fiverr for things like this, but I personally refer all of my clients to Lauren Harding & Dance Magick Media - www.dancemagickmedia.com)* & it doesn't have to be a huge financial investment. Depending on the genre/theme of your book, the style & tone of this video trailer can be used to convey that & draw in a new audience that may not have connected with your written or status social media posts. A book trailer is a great attention grabber for your website, social media & targeted ads.

- **Collaborations & Connections** – This is a broader idea because there really is NO limit to the collaborations & connections you can make. I love using Facebook Groups to look for targeted virtual book clubs that may be interested in adding your new book to their rotation, especially if you, the author, are willing to do a FB live Q&A with the group. Finding book bloggers that read & review books in your genre & offering them an advance copy can be another great way to make not only a connection for the future, but to reach another new audience that's already been developed by someone else.

Nurturing These Relationships

If we're going to stick with the online dating scenario, this step is once you've gained the interest of someone & are looking at if you might actually be a good match. This is where you want to make slightly more personal contact, still no pressure or expectations, but you're definitely inching closer to that first official date.

The best way to do this is by staying involved & engaged in those new connections you're making. These will usually be primarily online, so it means making sure that you're 'liking,' acknowledging, responding & engaging in comments & posts online. When you post to your social media, don't *post & ghost.'* Set a reminder on your calendar to check those posts & accounts 2 or 3 times a day *(I like to do this in the morning while enjoying my first cup of coffee, while nibbling lunch & before I unplug for the evening).*

For your new audience, receiving a 'heart' & quick reply to a comment means a TON & carries a lot of weight. This also means keeping up with your email correspondence, replying to messages you've received in response to the emails sent to your list, as well as correspondence regarding booking podcast interviews, possible book club connections, or collaboration opportunities.

Nothing ruins a new relationship more than going dark for a week or disappearing altogether. The world is huge but at the same time, one shitty experience can make that world real small, real quick. Nothing spreads faster than negative talk about an experience with someone we once admired. Don't be that person. Period.

Action!

It's time for that first coffee date! Put on your favorite authorly outfit *(let's be honest, chances are you're doing this from the comfort of your own home, so wear wtf you like)* & let's ask these new connections of yours for a little commitment. Nothing big like adopting a puppy or co-signing for a new condo, but something reasonable & completely within their interest, like preordering your book, attending an upcoming event, or participating in an online promotion you're running.

By this point, your big barrel filled with those original audience members has self-qualified themselves down through your funnel, to the spot where they get to decide if they're interested in you as an author, your brand & your book(s) enough to make that micro-commitment & whip out their credit card.

Now, you aren't just asking them for something; remember, you're offering them the amazing experience that comes from reading YOUR book. The literary creation you've been telling them about, teasing about & are now *(finally)* able to share, especially with THEM – your raving fans.

This is a great stage of the game to share testimonials you may have collected from advance-readers, industry professionals, hell, your mom & best friend from high school *(no one has to know)*. Readers *(just like you & I)* love to take the word of our people, other readers. *Trust me, receiving a review from someone about your book is like getting a golden ticket, one that you're going to want to show off whenever and however you can.*

Notes & Sparks of Genius:

_____

_____

_____

_____

_____

_____

_____

_____

_____

_____

_____

_____

_____

Notes & Sparks of Genius:

_____

_____

_____

_____

_____

_____

_____

_____

_____

_____

_____

_____

_____

_____

_____

_____

_____

_____

_____

_____

_____

_____

_____

_____

_____

Notes & Sparks of Genius:

Notes & Sparks of Genius:

_____

_____

_____

_____

_____

_____

_____

_____

_____

_____

_____

_____

_____

_____

_____

_____

_____

_____

_____

_____

_____

_____

_____

_____

_____

Notes & Sparks of Genius:

The Launch Timeline:
2-3 Months to Liftoff

When it comes to launching your book, it's always a great idea to start building excitement a few months in advance – that being said, it's never too late to start calling in your readers & sharing the magic of your literary creation. So, without further ado, let's dig in.

While you're still finishing your book, start brainstorming a list of fellow authors, professional colleagues, influencers, friends & mentors who you'd LOVE to have read an advance copy of your book *(this doesn't need to be printed & bound, a pdf manuscript is completely fine)* & receive a review from. Keep in mind, a lot of people are busy & won't be able to do this, BUT, this initial list is one filled with everyone you'd like to invite to participate & be a part of the excitement. It's a good idea to give these people between 3-4 weeks to read & provide you with a review. *More about this as well as researching podcast opportunities in a future section.*

One last note before you read on & most likely get a little overwhelmed or flustered – I've included a LOT of information & ideas here, but the best plan for YOU is going to be what feels right, works with your schedule, availability & desires. Keep in mind that if you're working with a professional publisher *(ahem)* they can help take care of quite a bit of this list for you.

My biggest recommendation is that you set & stick to a budget for your time, your attention, your energy & monetary investments. Take it from someone who's been down this road a time or two *(or 137)* & lost hours, days & a few $10's..*alright $50's...* more than planned because I wasn't keeping track of things as much as I'd have liked, allowing my irresponsible creative muse to take over & drive the bus.

2–3 Months Before Launch:
- Finalize your book title & cover design
- Create your ARC dream list
- Begin building buzz on social media (behind-the-scenes, writing journey)
- Set up your email list opt-in (freebie or teaser content)
- Update your author website (if applicable)
- Start researching potential podcasts & book bloggers

1–2 Months Before Launch:
- Send ARC emails & follow-ups
- Announce book title, cover sneak peeks & theme to your social media
- Start sending podcast outreach emails
- Create graphics for teasers, countdowns & quote posts
- Schedule social media content consistently

3–4 Weeks Before Launch:
- Confirm podcast guest spots & interviews
- Share early reader testimonials or blurbs
- Finalize book trailer *(if using one)*
- Plan launch week content *(giveaways, live Q&A, etc.)*
- Send a "coming soon" teaser to your email list

2–3 Weeks Before Launch:
- Begin a daily/near-daily book countdown on social media
- Highlight excerpts, reader reactions, reviews
- Share behind-the-scenes content *(your writing desk, nerves, snacks—anything!)*

1–2 Weeks Before Launch:
- Announce launch events or LIVEs
- Remind your email list that launch day is coming
- Create & schedule your launch day posts
- Draft your thank-you message to send post-launch

Launch Day!

- Celebrate online with a LIVE & heartfelt post
- Remind ARC readers to leave reviews
- Share testimonials, reader selfies & all the love
- THANK your audience via email, social, etc.

Post-Launch:

- Keep sharing content: reader reviews, book clubs, media
- Schedule even more podcasts/interviews
- Run a small giveaway or contest to keep momentum going
- Ask readers to recommend the book to a friend or club
- Reflect & plan next steps!

Notes & Sparks of Genius:

_____

_____

_____

_____

_____

_____

_____

_____

_____

_____

_____

_____

_____

_____

_____

Notes & Sparks of Genius:

Notes & Sparks of Genius:

_____
_____
_____
_____
_____
_____
_____
_____
_____
_____
_____
_____
_____
_____
_____
_____
_____
_____
_____
_____
_____
_____
_____
_____
_____
_____

Notes & Sparks of Genius:

_____

_____

_____

_____

_____

_____

_____

_____

_____

_____

_____

_____

_____

_____

_____

_____

_____

_____

_____

_____

_____

_____

_____

_____

Planning Your Official Book Launch/Signing

A book launch/signing can be a great way to meet your readers face-to-face, as well as to connect with new readers & supporters. While it may seem overwhelming at first glance, I've included a quick cheat sheet below that will help take the worst headaches out of what can be a phenomenal & memorable experience for you & your readers. It's also a great idea to chat with your publisher to see about placing a preorder for books to have available at the event.

Step 1: Pick Your Vibe + Venue

What kind of event do you have in mind?
- Casual celebration *(coffee shop or local bookstore hangout)*
- Formal reading + Q&A *(library, gallery, or event space)*
- Interactive/signing + mingle *(community center, boutique, winery)*
- Virtual launch *(Instagram Live, Zoom, Facebook Live)*

Venue ideas:
- Independent bookstores *(start local!)*
- Coffee shops, cafes, breweries or vineyards
- Libraries or community centers
- Art studios, coworking spaces, or yoga studios
- Your own backyard or a friend's cozy space
- Online *(Zoom, StreamYard, IG or FB Live)*

Step 2: Choose Your Date & Time

Give yourself at least **3–4 weeks of lead time to promote the event.**

Timing tips:
- Evenings/weekends tend to get a better turnout.
- Consider school schedules, holidays, or local events that may conflict.
- If you're virtual, choose a time your audience is most active.

Step 3: What Will You Do at the Event?

Keep it simple, fun, and true to you, but also keep in mind that having a tentative schedule helps your guests know what to expect.

Here's a sample flow:

1. Welcome + intro *(2–3 min)*
2. Short reading from the book *(5–10 min)*
3. Author Q&A or behind-the-scenes stories *(10–15 min)*
4. Book signing or meet-and-greet *(1-2 hours)*
5. *Optional:* Light refreshments, giveaways, or book-themed activities

Virtual? Add a giveaway, invite a special guest, or host a live Q&A with your audience.

Step 4: Bring the Essentials

Must-haves:

- Copies of your book *(Preordered copies as well as extras to sell at the event)*
- Sharpies or your favorite pens for signing books
- Cash/change & digital payment options *(Venmo, PayPal, Square, CashApp)*
- Business cards or bookmarks *(something that shows people how to stay in touch with you quickly & easily)*
- Tablecloth & display materials *(stand-up sign, easel, book stands)*
- A friend/helper to manage the table, signing line & take pics

Step 5: Promote the Event

Post about your event on:

- Social media *(start 3–4 weeks out)*
- Your email list
- Local event calendars or Facebook Groups
- Collaborating venue's page *(they may share your promo too)*
- Canva posters/flyers for local businesses, libraries, coffee shops

Pro tip: Create a simple RSVP, FB Event, or Eventbrite link to get a headcount

Bonus Fun Ideas

- A Raffle or Giveaway – *enter to win a signed copy, bookish goodies, or a gift card*
- Photo Op Spot – *a cute backdrop or banner for selfies*
- Local Collaborations – *invite a musician, artist, or another author to join you*
- Themed snacks or drinks based on your book vibe - *either bring with you or work with your venue to create something special*
- Another fun idea is to have your own copy of your new book available for those in attendance to sign YOUR book. This not only gives your community a chance to be personally involved in your day, but a keepsake for you to look back on such a monumental experience in the future.

Final Tips

- Don't overthink it—it's about connection, not perfection.
- Ask a friend to help manage details or capture behind-the-scenes moments.
- If you're working with a professional publisher, they can often be hired to attend these events to help manage details, man your book sales table & act as your biggest-fan *after your mom/dad of course*
- Take a deep breath & ENJOY the moment. **You wrote a whole damn book—celebrate it!**

Notes & Sparks of Genius:

_____

_____

_____

_____

_____

_____

_____

_____

Notes & Sparks of Genius:

Plan Your Official Book Launch/Signing Event:

What kind of event do you have in mind?

_____

_____

_____

Venue ideas?

_____

_____

_____

Possible Date & Times?

_____

_____

_____

Outline a sample flow for your event:

_____

_____

_____

_____

_____

_____

_____

_____

_____

Make a list of what you'll want to bring:

_____

_____

_____

_____

_____

_____

_____

_____

_____

_____

How will you promote your event? Do you have any friends/family/colleagues who can help promote it to their audiences?

_____

_____

_____

_____

_____

_____

_____

_____

_____

_____

_____

Any other notes to remember while planning your event:

_____

_____

_____

_____

_____

_____

_____

_____

_____

_____

_____

_____

_____

_____

_____

_____

_____

_____

_____

_____

_____

_____

_____

_____

_____

_____

_____

_____

Notes & Sparks of Genius:

_____
_____
_____
_____
_____
_____
_____
_____
_____
_____
_____
_____
_____
_____
_____
_____
_____
_____
_____
_____
_____
_____
_____
_____
_____

Visibility & Voice: Authentic Outreach to Maximize Buzz

What's an ARC Reader & Why Do You Want Them in Your Corner?

ARC stands for Advance Reader Copy—aka the sneak peek squad who gets to read your book before it's officially released. These magical humans are often your first readers, first reviewers & first raving fans. Think of ARC readers as your literary hype team. Their job? Read the book early, leave an honest review on launch day *(or as close to it as possible)* & help create an authentic buzz so your book shows up looking fabulous & well-loved right out the gate.

Why does this matter? Because social proof sells books. Reviews help build trust & visibility, especially for indie or first-time authors. Readers want to know someone else has read your book & loved it, or at least found it meaningful, spicy, heartfelt, or hilarious. ARC reviews give your book a boost on platforms like Amazon & GoodReads & make it easier for new readers to say *"HELL YES!"* when they see that other folks have already said *"HELL YES."*

Finding ARC readers doesn't have to be hard or awkward. Start with your email list, social media followers, writing groups, or book-loving friends. You can post in Facebook groups for readers in your genre, or use platforms like BookSirens or StoryOrigin if you want something more automated. Qualify them by asking a few simple questions: *Do you regularly leave reviews? What genres do you love? Can you commit to reading and reviewing by a specific date?* Be clear about expectations & remember, once again, it's about building relationships, not just passing out free copies of your new wordy creation. Treat your ARC readers like the VIPs they are & many of them will stick around long after launch day.

I've included a sample email template that can be used when contacting prospective ARC readers, as well as a few sleaze-free DM ideas & social media posts that can be used to drum up interest from your existing audience of FB friends & followers.

Notes & Sparks of Genius:

Sample Email for ARC Reader Outreach

Subject: Want an early peek at my new book?

Hey [First Name],

So... I wrote a book. (!!)

It's been a wild, beautiful, slightly terrifying ride—but I'm thrilled to finally share it with the world soon. Before launch day officially arrives, I'm looking for a handful of readers to get a sneak peek & share an honest review if they feel called to.

Here's the deal:

- You'll get an advance digital copy of the book *(PDF or ePub)*.
- You read it before launch day *(no pressure, just love)*.
- If you enjoy it, I'd be grateful for a review on Amazon, Goodreads, or even a shout-out on social media.

Early reviews help more than most people realize—especially for a newer author like me just stepping into the publishing world.

If you're in, just reply to this email & I'll send the early copy your way!

Thank you so much for your support—it truly means the world.

With big bookish love,

[Your Name]
[Website or socials if you want to include]

Write Your Own Email for ARC Reader Outreach:

NON-Sleazy DM Templates for ARC Readers

Option 1:

Hey [Name]! I'm getting ready to launch my book (!!) and I'm looking for a few early readers to check it out and maybe leave a quick review. Totally no pressure, but I'd love to send you a copy if you're interested!

Option 2:

Hi [Name], I've got a book coming out soon and I'm sharing early copies with a small group of readers to help build buzz. If you'd like to read it early and leave a review, I'd be thrilled to send you the PDF!

Option 3:

Hey [Name], I know you're a fellow book lover—would you be up for reading an advance copy of my new book before it launches? I'd be super grateful for a review or even just some early feedback. Let me know!

Write your own:

_____

_____

_____

_____

_____

_____

_____

_____

Notes & Sparks of Genius:

NON-Sleazy Facebook Post Templates for ARC Readers

Post Option 1:

Hey book lovers! 💚

I'm a new author getting ready to launch my book [Title] in just a few weeks, and I'm putting together a small group of advance readers to check it out early.

It's [a quick one-liner about the genre, vibe, or hook—e.g., "a cozy romance with a little sass and a lot of heart"]. If you'd be interested in reading the early copy (PDF) and leaving an honest review, I'd love to send it your way.

Drop a ✏ or DM me if you're curious and I'll send the details!

Post Option 2:

ARC Readers Wanted! 📚✦

If you love [insert your genre—ex: spicy paranormal romance / uplifting memoirs / twisty thrillers] and discovering books before they launch, I've got something for you!

I'm offering a sneak peek of my debut, [Title], to a handful of early readers. All I ask in return is an honest review on Amazon or Goodreads. Want to help a new author out and get first dibs on a new read?

Comment below or shoot me a message! 🙏

Post Option 3:

📢 ARC READER CALL!

My book baby is almost here, and I'm building a small advance reader crew to help me share it with the world.

The story is [1–2 sentence teaser: genre, emotional hook, or "if you liked ___, you might love ___"].

If you're up for reading an early digital copy and leaving a short review when it launches, I'd be so grateful. Think of it as being part of the book's birth party 🎉

Comment below or message me if you're in—I'll send over the details!

Write your own:

_____

_____

_____

_____

_____

_____

_____

_____

_____

_____

_____

_____

_____

_____

_____

_____

_____

Notes & Sparks of Genius:

Notes & Sparks of Genius:

Podcasting: A New Author's Secret Weapon

Podcasts are one of the most powerful *(& totally underrated)* ways to build buzz around your book, especially if you're a new author without a giant following or big-budget ad plan. When you're a guest on a podcast, you're essentially borrowing the host's audience & getting to talk about your book, your story & your message in a warm, human way. Listeners get to hear your voice, your energy, your excitement & your why, which builds trust faster than any static post ever will. Plus, podcast episodes live forever online, so your interview can keep attracting readers long after launch day.

The best part? You don't need to be "famous" to get booked on podcasts. You just need to be a good fit with the show, host & their audience of listeners. Start by looking for podcasts that align with your book's themes, target audience, or your personal story. For example, if you write cozy mysteries, look for podcasts that highlight mystery authors or avid readers. If your memoir touches on healing, creativity, or resilience, seek out mental wellness, self-help, or inspirational shows.

A few great ways to find a plethora of podcasts is to search Apple Podcasts, Spotify, or directories like Podmatch. You can also check out any number of free Facebook groups that are filled with podcast hosts & managers. One Facebook group that I've used a number of times for myself & my clients is: '**_Podcast Guest Collaboration Community - Find a Guest, Be a Guest_**.' *(which has nearly 74k members currently)*.

Once you've found a podcast you're interested in, follow the show & hosts on social media, listen to a few episodes & get a feel for their vibe before reaching out. Be sure to personalize your communication, share who you are, what your book is about & how you think their listeners would benefit from you being a guest. I recommend that my clients provide a few juicy talking points tying in something relevant to a recent episode, so the podcast host can easily see how you'll fit into their program.

I've included a tracker for you to compile your dream podcast opportunties, a sample email template that can be used when contacting prospective podcasts, as well as a few sleaze-free DM ideas to get you going.

Notes & Sparks of Genius:

Dream Podcast Outreach Tracker

Podcast Name:

_____

Podcast Host/Booking Contact:

_____

Proposed Topic to Discuss:

_____

Date Contacted/Followed-up:

_____

Podcast Booked/Recorded/Released:

_____

Podcast Name:

_____

Podcast Host/Booking Contact:

_____

Proposed Topic to Discuss:

_____

Date Contacted/Followed-up:

_____

Podcast Booked/Recorded/Released:

_____

Podcast Name:

_____

Podcast Host/Booking Contact:

_____

Proposed Topic to Discuss:

_____

Date Contacted/Followed-up:

_____

Podcast Booked/Recorded/Released:

_____

Podcast Name:

_____

Podcast Host/Booking Contact:

_____

Proposed Topic to Discuss:

_____

Date Contacted/Followed-up:

_____

Podcast Booked/Recorded/Released:

_____

Podcast Name:

_____

Podcast Host/Booking Contact:

_____

Proposed Topic to Discuss:

_____

Date Contacted/Followed-up:

_____

Podcast Booked/Recorded/Released:

_____

Podcast Name:

_____

Podcast Host/Booking Contact:

_____

Proposed Topic to Discuss:

_____

Date Contacted/Followed-up:

_____

Podcast Booked/Recorded/Released:

_____

Podcast Name:

_____

Podcast Host/Booking Contact:

_____

Proposed Topic to Discuss:

_____

Date Contacted/Followed-up:

_____

Podcast Booked/Recorded/Released:

_____

Podcast Name:

_____

Podcast Host/Booking Contact:

_____

Proposed Topic to Discuss:

_____

Date Contacted/Followed-up:

_____

Podcast Booked/Recorded/Released:

_____

Podcast Name:

_____

Podcast Host/Booking Contact:

_____

Proposed Topic to Discuss:

_____

Date Contacted/Followed-up:

_____

Podcast Booked/Recorded/Released:

_____

Podcast Name:

_____

Podcast Host/Booking Contact:

_____

Proposed Topic to Discuss:

_____

Date Contacted/Followed-up:

_____

Podcast Booked/Recorded/Released:

_____

Podcast Name:

_____

Podcast Host/Booking Contact:

_____

Proposed Topic to Discuss:

_____

Date Contacted/Followed-up:

_____

Podcast Booked/Recorded/Released:

_____

Podcast Name:

_____

Podcast Host/Booking Contact:

_____

Proposed Topic to Discuss:

_____

Date Contacted/Followed-up:

_____

Podcast Booked/Recorded/Released:

_____

Subject: Podcast Guest Pitch: [Book Title]

Hi [Podcast Host Name],

My name's [Your Name], and I'm a [genre] author getting ready to launch my new book, *[Book Title]*—a story that [quick one-liner about theme or emotional hook].

I'm reaching out because I'd love to be a guest on your podcast to talk about [your genre/topic/theme], the messy magic of writing a first book, and what it's been like to bring this project to life.

A few topics I'd love to explore on your show:

- [Personal topic or theme from your book—e.g., "What writing this story taught me about healing"]
- [Craft or genre-based topic—e.g., "How fiction helped me rewrite old narratives"]
- [Something more personal/quirky—e.g., "How writing in coffee shops with bad Wi-Fi saved my book"]

I know your audience loves real, honest conversations—and that's exactly what I bring to the mic. If it feels like a fit, I'd be thrilled to chat more!

Thanks so much for the work you're doing to support writers, storytellers, and big conversations.

With gratitude,

[Your Name]
[Website / IG handle / other link]

Write Your Own Email for Podcast Host/Guesting Outreach

NON-Sleazy DM Templates for Podcast Hosts

Option 1:

Hi [Host Name]! I'm a new author getting ready to launch my debut book and would love to be a guest on your podcast if you're booking! I can speak on [topic or theme] and think your audience would really enjoy it. Can I send you more info?

Option 2:

Hey [Host Name], big fan of your podcast! I just finished writing my book [Title] and would love to be a guest to chat about [topic or angle that fits their show]. Let me know if you're looking for guests—I'd love to connect!

Option 3:

Hi [Name], I'm reaching out because your podcast aligns so beautifully with the themes in my upcoming book. I'd be honored to be a guest and share a bit about the writing journey and what readers can expect. Can I send you more details?

Write your own:

_____

_____

_____

_____

_____

_____

_____

Notes & Sparks of Genius:

NON-Sleazy Facebook Post Templates for Podcast Guesting Opportunities

Post Option 1:

Hey podcast hosts & collab-minded creators
I'm a debut author gearing up to launch my book, [Title], and I'm looking to do a few interviews over the next few weeks!
If your podcast touches on [insert topic—e.g., creativity, books, mindset, entrepreneurship, storytelling], I'd love to chat about my book journey, the writing process, and some real behind-the-scenes moments from launching my first book.
Let me know if you're looking for guests—I'd love to connect and bring value to your audience!

Post Option 2:

Hi there! I'm a new author looking to connect with podcast hosts who love talking books, creativity, or the messy magic of following big dreams.
My book, [Title], is [genre + quick 1-liner about the vibe—ex: "a raw and honest memoir about surviving burnout and rediscovering purpose"].
I'd love to be a guest on your podcast to talk about:
- What writing this book taught me
- [Theme or takeaway from the book]
- Or anything your audience might resonate with

Happy to send more info or a media one-sheet. Just drop a comment or message me!

Post Option 3:

Hey hosts! I'm a new author launching my book soon and looking for podcast spots to share the journey. I speak on [topics or themes] and love real, open convo around creativity, resilience, and storytelling.
Drop your show link below if you're booking guests! Would love to connect 🎙️ ✦

Write your own:

_____

_____

_____

_____

_____

_____

_____

_____

_____

_____

_____

_____

_____

_____

_____

_____

_____

_____

_____

_____

_____

Notes & Sparks of Genius:

Notes & Sparks of Genius:

Book Blogger & Book Club Outreach

Book bloggers & book clubs are like the fairy godmothers of the reader world, sharing books they love, spreading the word with passion & building tight-knit communities of fellow book lovers. For a new author, these groups can be a game-changer when it comes to visibility, social proof & word-of-mouth momentum. A single rave review on a blogger's site or an enthusiastic group discussion in a book club can lead to new fans, new reviews & even new opportunities you hadn't imagined *(like speaking gigs, collabs, or bonus sales long after launch).*

To find the right *(and legit)* book bloggers, start with your genre & a good old-fashioned Google or Pinterest search. Typing in something as simple as *"[Your Genre] book bloggers"* or *"[Your Genre] book review blogs"* will often result in a quick list of bloggers looking for new reads. Once you've found a few, do your own *vibe check*, visit their site or social media, see if they're active & look for submission guidelines *(most bloggers have a review request form).* Be respectful, personalize your pitch & always offer a free copy of your book—no strings attached.

For book clubs, you can tap into both virtual & local spaces. Facebook Groups are full of niche reader clubs, especially for specific genres, diverse reads, or author Q&A sessions. You can also check with your local library, bookstore, or community center to find in-person clubs. Offer to attend *(virtually or in person)*, host a Q&A, or send along discussion questions. Most clubs are excited to support new authors & let's be honest, having a book club chat about your story is the ultimate full-circle moment.

I've included a sample email template that can be used when contacting prospective bloggers or book clubs, as well as a few sleaze-free DM ideas & social media posts to help get you going. Be sure to customize & personalize these to match your voice & tone.

Notes & Sparks of Genius:

Sample Email for Book Blogger & Book Club Outreach

Subject: New Book Release-Would Love to Share with Your Readers!

Hi [Name]!

I hope this note finds you cozied up with a great read & your favorite beverage. I'm reaching out because I'm a newly published author & I just released my [genre] book titled [Book Title]. It's full of [insert 2–3 juicy descriptors—ex: "small-town magic, found family & one slightly haunted antique shop"] & I think it might be a great fit for your blog/audience/book club.

I'd be honored if you'd consider reading it & possibly sharing your thoughts with your community. I'm more than happy to provide a free digital copy & if you're open to it, I'd love to send along a few discussion questions or even pop into a book club chat (virtually or in person) to answer questions or spill a little behind-the-scenes tea.

Let me know if you're interested & I'll send everything your way!

Thanks for all you do to support new authors & get great books into the hands of readers.

Warmly,

[Your Name]

[Optional: website or link to book info]
[Optional: social handle or email signature]

Write Your Own Email for Book Blogger & Book Club Outreach:

NON-Sleazy DM Templates for Book Bloggers & Book Clubs

Option 1:

Hey [Name]! I just released my first book ([Book Title]) & would LOVE to get it into the hands of a few readers who enjoy [insert genre or vibe—ex: "feel-good contemporary romance with a little sass & heart"]. I've been following your reviews & thought it might be a fun fit! Want me to send over the info?

Option 2:

Hi there! I just published a new [genre] novel called [Book Title] & I'm reaching out to a few awesome book clubs who might want to check it out! I'd be happy to send a free digital copy & discussion questions if you're up for it. If your group decides to give it a read, I'd even love to join in for a virtual chat or Q&A! Would your group be interested?

Option 3:

Hi! I'm a new author & just released a book I'm super proud of—[Book Title]. I'm reaching out to see if you'd be open to receiving a free copy to review or consider for your book club! No pressure, I just wanted to share in case it's your kind of story. Let me know!

Write your own:

_____

_____

_____

_____

_____

_____

_____

Notes & Sparks of Genius:

NON-Sleazy Facebook Post Templates for Book Blogger & Book Club Opportunities

Post Option 1:

New Author Alert! ✨📚

Hi book lovers! I'm a first-time author & just released my debut [genre] novel, [Book Title]—a story full of [insert quick teaser: "small-town charm, spicy secrets & one bookish heroine who's done playing small"]. I'm currently looking for:

- Book bloggers or reviewers open to reading a free copy
- Book clubs (*virtual or local*) that love fresh stories & fun author Q&As

If you or your group might be interested in checking it out, I'd LOVE to send a digital copy your way! No pressure, just sharing the love & hoping to find some amazing new readers.

Drop a comment or DM me, and I'll send over the details!

Post Option 2:

Calling all readers, reviewers & bookish badasses! 🕵️‍♀️📖📚

I've just published my first book ([Book Title]) & am putting together a small team of ARC readers, bloggers & book clubbers who want to dive in early & help me spread the word.

- ✨ You'll get a free copy.
- ✨ I'll love you forever.
- ✨ There may be bonus goodies involved. ✦✦

If you enjoy [insert a few relevant tags/themes: "slow-burn romance, strong female leads, or ghostly plot twists"], this one's for you!

Let me know below or shoot me a DM if you're down to read & review!

Post Option 3:

📖 BOOK CLUB FRIENDS! 📖

Hey y'all—I'm a new author & my debut [genre] novel [Book Title] just launched! I'm currently looking for a few book clubs (virtual or in-person) who might be interested in reading it for an upcoming pick! The story includes:

💬 Great discussion-worthy themes

🐩 An author who's down to join your Q&A (virtually or local if nearby!)

🖤 A free digital copy & optional discussion guide

If that sounds like a fun fit for your group, I'd be thrilled to send it your way. Just comment below or message me and we'll make it happen!

Write your own:

_____

_____

_____

_____

_____

_____

_____

_____

_____

_____

_____

_____

_____

_____

Notes & Sparks of Genius:

Notes & Sparks of Genius:

Cross-Promotion Magic

Writing can often feel like a solo adventure, but launching a book doesn't have to be. In fact, one of the smartest *(& most fun)* things you can do as a new author is cross-promote with other creatives, coaches, service providers, or fellow authors who align with your vibe & your audience.

Cross-promotion is all about sharing the spotlight, expanding each other's reach & making a bigger impact together. Whether it's a mutual shoutout, a shared giveaway, or a joint Instagram Live, collaboration can take your launch from *"just me over here screaming into the void"* to *"hey, look who's talking about my book!"*

Start by looking for natural overlap: *Do you know any authors in your genre or niche? Are there coaches, podcasters, or bloggers who serve your ideal readers? Maybe you're friends with an artist, tarot reader, or speaker who'd love to swap features or freebies.* The key is to find people who complement your message or mission, rather than competing with it. Then, get creative. Host a joint giveaway. Do a *"Day in the Life"* Instagram takeover for each other. Shout each other out in your email newsletters. Recommend one another's books. You can even bundle your book with someone else's offer *(think: "read this book and grab a guided journal from my soul-sister friend")*.

The bottom line: collaboration builds community, and community sells books in a way that's aligned, authentic & way more fun than trying to do it all yourself. So don't be afraid to reach out, connect & find your launch-day hype crew. *(Bonus: these connections often last way longer than a single promo & lead to some seriously magical friendships.)*

On the next few pages, I've included a smattering of cross-promotion ideas for a variety of genres. Keep in mind that these are just the tip of the iceberg & the world is your oyster. So... have fun!

Notes & Sparks of Genius:

Cross-Promotion Ideas

For All Genres:

- **Author Buddy Book Bundle:** Team up with 1–2 authors in a similar or complementary genre and offer a bundle giveaway *(signed copies, bonus downloads, etc.)*.
- **Podcast Guest Swaps:** You guest on their show, they guest on yours *(or your IG Live)*.
- **Shared Email Newsletter Feature:** Highlight each other in a reader email with *"If you liked my book, you'll love hers..."*
- **Bookish Instagram Live or Facebook Q&A:** Chat about your writing journey, themes & answer questions together.
- **Cross-Promo Printable Swap:** You offer a bonus printable from them *(like journaling prompts, coloring pages, or worksheets)* & they do the same with your goodies.
- **Joint Giveaway for Book Clubs:** Include multiple authors, free copies & a group Zoom Q&A.
- **Reel or TikTok Collabs:** Record a short *"pass the pen"* or *"writer/reader life"* style video that each of you posts to your own audience.

Fiction : *Perfect Pairings here are other authors in your genre (or adjacent ones), artists, character illustrators, bookstagrammers, fan art creators, etc.*

- **Character Swap Interview:** You write an interview with their character, and they do the same with yours.
- **Reader Gift Bundle:** Offer your book + their themed merch (candles, bookmarks, etc.) in a giveaway.
- **Pinterest or Spotify Collab:** Share mood boards or playlists inspired by your stories and tag each other.
- **Virtual Reading Night:** You each read an excerpt live and chat about what inspired the scenes.

Memoir: *Perfect Pairings here are coaches, podcasters, therapists, speakers, or fellow memoirists with related life experiences.*

- **Real Talk IG Series:** Share short video convos about your journeys, trauma, healing, creativity, etc.
- **Companion Resource Swap:** Offer a workbook, journal prompt set, or printable that pairs with your story, created by or in collab with another expert.
- **Story Swap:** Invite others to share short pieces about how your story or topic has impacted them & do the same for theirs.

Non-Fiction: *Perfect Pairings here are bloggers, speakers, coaches, educators, or other authors in similar themes (personal development, parenting, relationships, etc.)*

- **Workshop Swap:** Co-host a mini-class or Zoom talk that connects your book with their expertise.
- **Expert Roundup Blog Post:** Feature quotes from your network (& your book) & let everyone share it.
- **Checklist or Quiz Exchange:** Create short, shareable tools that link to both of your offers/websites.

Self-Help / Personal Growth: *Perfect Pairings here are coaches, therapists, healers, mindset mentors & anyone who serves your same audience from a different angle.*

- **"Growth Glow-Up" Bundle:** Your book & their audio meditation or journal & a guided challenge.
- **Email Challenge Swap:** Run a 5-day challenge together *(Ex: "5 Days to Unblock Your Magic")* that features both of your content.
- **Social Media Series:** Collaborate on a short series, like *"3 Lessons That Changed My Life,"* each of you posts your own & tags the other.

Business/Leadership: *Perfect Pairings here are consultants, coaches, podcasters, LinkedIn creators, productivity experts, or SaaS platforms/tools.*

- **LinkedIn Live or Webinar Collab:** Co-host a "Lunch & Learn" session.
- **Lead Magnet Boost:** Add your book to a business toolkit or bundle being offered by a peer.
- **Testimonial Trade:** Write blurbs for each other's books or offers, especially if they align or reference similar ideas.

Write your own:

_____

_____

_____

_____

_____

_____

_____

_____

_____

_____

_____

_____

_____

_____

_____

_____

_____

_____

_____

Notes & Sparks of Genius:

Book Trailer Videos

Think of a book trailer video as the movie preview for your literary masterpiece. It's a short, attention-grabbing visual that teases the vibe, voice & heart of your book in a way that stops the scroll & pulls people in. Whether you're writing fiction, memoir, or non-fiction, a well-made trailer helps potential readers feel something before they've even cracked the cover. It builds anticipation, sets the tone for your brand as an author & gives your audience something exciting to share. Plus, videos tend to perform better on social media & this gives you a fresh, visual way to promote your book without saying, *"Hey, buy my book"* for the tenth time that week.

You don't need a Hollywood budget to make it work, either; plenty of book trailers are created with tools like Canva, CapCut, or by Fiverr freelancers. I personally refer all of my clients to Lauren Harding & Dance Magick Media - www.dancemagickmedia.com. She's a true magician when it comes to turning words (whether they be books, lyrics, or something else entirely) into visual gold.

The magic comes from matching the style of the video to the energy of your book. Whether you're aiming for spine-tingling suspense, soulful reflection, or laugh-out-loud sass, your trailer becomes a powerful part of your launch strategy & a tool you can reuse on your website, in your email list, in pitches to podcasts or press & across every social platform you're active on.

Creative Book Trailer Video Ideas:

- **Vibe Check Montage:** Pair background music with a mix of short phrases from your book, dramatic keywords, or quotes. Overlay them on moody images or B-roll that matches the story's energy.

- **Voiceover Teaser:** Record yourself reading a paragraph or two from the book *(or hire a voice actor if you'd rather not)*. Overlay with visuals or stock footage.

- **Behind-the-Scenes Peek:** Show your writing process, your messy notebook, that one cozy café where it all started & invite people to experience a small part of your creative journey.

- **Character or Theme Spotlight:** For fiction, highlight a key character or scene. For non-fiction or memoir, tease a core lesson or *"aha moment."*

- **Countdown Trailer:** Use a simple countdown & exciting visuals to build hype *("5 days until launch")* & share sneak peeks each day.

- **Text-Only Teaser:** Keep it super simple with just music & animated text revealing your hook or blurb line-by-line. Short, bold & effective.

Notes & Sparks of Genius:

_____

_____

_____

_____

_____

_____

_____

_____

_____

_____

_____

_____

_____

_____

_____

_____

_____

_____

_____

Giveaways & Contests

Finally, if you're looking to build genuine excitement around your book without shouting "BUY MY BOOK" from every rooftop, giveaways & contests are a brilliant way to create buzz, build visibility & expand your reach, especially when you're just getting started. People love free stuff, but more than that, they love the chance to be a part of something exciting & new. Hosting a giveaway makes your audience feel involved, appreciated & it gives them an easy reason to engage with your content, share your work, or even preorder your book.

You don't need to give away a trip to Bali to make an impact. The real magic comes from offering something aligned with your book, your voice & your reader's interests. Whether you're giving away a signed copy, a bundle of themed goodies, or a character named after the winner *(yes, really)*, contests are a fun & authentic way to get people talking. *Bonus: they're also an excellent tool for growing your email list, boosting social engagement & even partnering with other authors or creators for cross-promotion.*

Creative Giveaway & Contest Ideas:

- **Signed Book & Bookish Goodies:** Include a copy of your book, a cozy candle, themed bookmarks, or your favorite writing snack.

- **"Name a Character" Contest:** Perfect for fiction authors working on the next book, invite readers to suggest names! There are a few fairly famous authors who run super successful contests for readers to be able to name the victims or killers in their next book.

- **Reader Review Raffle:** Anyone who posts a review *(Amazon, Goodreads, social)* gets entered to win a bonus prize.

- **Fan Art or Fan Quote Contest:** Invite readers to draw a scene, share a favorite quote, or create a themed playlist based on your book.

- **Preorder Party Giveaway:** Everyone who preorders the book gets entered to win a VIP goodie bag or an exclusive bonus chapter.

- **Collab Contest:** Team up with a fellow author or creative business & bundle both your books or products into one juicy giveaway.

- **"Tell a Friend" Challenge:** Ask followers to tag or share with a friend who'd love your book for a chance to win a copy for both of them!

Notes & Sparks of Genius:

_____

_____

_____

_____

_____

_____

_____

_____

_____

_____

_____

_____

_____

_____

_____

_____

_____

_____

_____

_____

_____

Wrap Up: You've Got This

Let's take a moment & just breathe together, okay?

You've done something that most people only talk about. You wrote a book. You've published a book. And now, you're learning how to share it with the world in a way that feels aligned, exciting & authentic to YOU. That's no small thing, friend. You deserve a standing ovation, a jumbo-cupcake & maybe even a nap. But before you log off & dive into your next chapter *(pun absolutely intended)*, let's land this plane with a little love & a few final thoughts.

First & foremost, this isn't about perfection. It never was. There's no one-size-fits-all marketing plan or magical blueprint to becoming a bestselling author overnight. What does matter is showing up consistently, listening to your gut & staying connected to the heart of why you wrote this book in the first place. Your story matters. Your voice matters. And the way you show up for your readers? That creates a ripple effect you may never fully see, but I promise, it's real & once started, it will continue on for all eternity.

As you move forward, keep track of what feels good & what works for you. That might be a particular platform, a kind of post, a podcast appearance, or something wild & random that surprises you. When something doesn't work? Adjust. Tweak. PIVOT! *(Friends, anyone?!)* Try again. Or leave it behind & try something totally new. Your author journey is going to evolve & that's a beautiful thing. The goal isn't to do this "right" according to someone else's checklist, it's to build a book life that feels like YOU.

Whether you're shouting your book from the rooftops or whispering it into the right inboxes, remember: ***you are doing amazing***. This is just the beginning. Keep connecting, keep learning, keep creating & most of all, keep trusting that your words were meant to be read. Your story was meant to be told.

Now go on. The world needs what you wrote.

Note: If you haven't yet published your book, flip to the next page for details on how you can work with a hybrid publishing pro to ensure that your book-baby is presented to the world like the masterpiece it is.

Notes & Sparks of Genius:

Megs Thompson is an Intuitive Writing Coach, Word-Twerking Book-Doula, Ghostwriter, Editor, Publisher & all-around Storytelling Sorceress. While she originally hails from the rain-soaked Pacific Northwest, Megs now calls the wild of Montana home, with her husband & their menagerie of four-legged, fur-covered children.

Megs has known since the age of 7 that her purpose in life is to help others not only recognize the value within their personal stories & lived experiences, but to then deliver those stories to the world through professionally published books.

Through her businesses, **megswrites llc** & **in omnia paratus publishing llc**, Megs spends her days supporting, coaching, empowering & encouraging creative individuals as they move confidently through the often messy & uncomfortable minefield of their personal healing process to uncover the magic & strength hidden within their unique life stories.

TLDR Version: Megs coaches YOU to see your personal stories for the magic they contain, by helping YOU get out of your own way, holding you accountable & cheering you on like an over-invested dance mom. But in a really good way.

For more information about how to work with Megs, visit her websites @ www.megswrites.com & www.inomniaparatuspublishing.com or visit her socials by scanning the provided QR code.

www.ingramcontent.com/pod-product-compliance
Lightning Source LLC
Chambersburg PA
CBHW051324120626
46547CB00015B/2387